ESCAPING TITANIC

A YOUNG GIRL'S TRUE STORY OF SURVIVAL

BY MARYBETH LORBIECKI   ILLUSTRATED BY KORY S. HEINZEN

PICTURE WINDOW BOOKS
a capstone imprint

Thanks to our advisers for their expertise, research, and advice:

Norm Lewis, President/Founder/CEO
Canadian Titanic Society

Terry Flaherty, PhD, Professor of English
Minnesota State University, Mankato

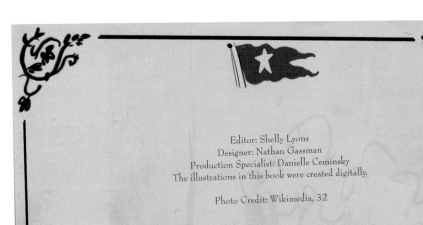

Editor: Shelly Lyons
Designer: Nathan Gassman
Production Specialist: Danielle Ceminsky
The illustrations in this book were created digitally.

Photo Credit: Wikimedia, 32

Picture Window Books
1710 Roe Crest Drive
North Mankato, MN 56003
www.capstonepub.com

Library of Congress Cataloging-in-Publication Data
Lorbiecki, Marybeth.
Escaping titanic : a young girl's true story of survival /
written by Marybeth Lorbiecki and illustrated by Kory S. Heinzen.
p. cm.
ISBN 978-1-4048-7143-4 (library binding)
ISBN 978-1-4048-7235-6 (paperback)
1. Becker, Ruth Elizabeth, 1899-1990—Juvenile literature.
2. Titanic (Steamship)—Juvenile literature. 3. Denver
(Colo.)—Biography—Juvenile literature. I. Heinzen, Kory II. Title.
CT275.B43L67 2012
978.8'83031092—dc23
[B]
                                        2011030158

Printed in the United States of America in North Mankato, Minnesota.
042013   007329R

On a train from London, 12-year-old Ruth Becker spied the RMS *Titanic*.

It rose like a city on the sea, 11 stories high and four blocks long. It was the biggest, fanciest, most expensive ship ever made—built to be unsinkable!

But to Ruth, the *Titanic* was just another ship. And after a month at sea, Ruth was sick of ships.

Ruth missed her warm home in India and her father. He was a missionary and had to stay behind. In her coat pocket, Ruth kept safe the handkerchief he had given her.

Two mighty whistles blasted. Time to board!

Ruth and her 4-year-old sister, Marion, eyed the other passengers. The first-class women strolled aboard with their furs and hats. Nearby trudged the third-class families in scarves and caps and boots.

Once aboard, Mother held baby Richard tight. She pulled an officer aside. "I'm not one bit happy about being on this ship!" she told him. "I'm nervous because this is its first trip."

Ruth sighed. Must Mother *always* worry?

"The *Titanic* has watertight compartments, and if anything does happen, they'll keep the ship up until we get help," the man said.

While Mother fretted, Ruth and Marion ran ahead to find their cabin on Deck F.

Ruth had never seen such riches! The ceramic sink bowls sparkled, the carved wooden beds gleamed, and the crisp new sheets smelled like flowers.

She noticed how the ship's engines hummed like the grasshoppers back home in India.

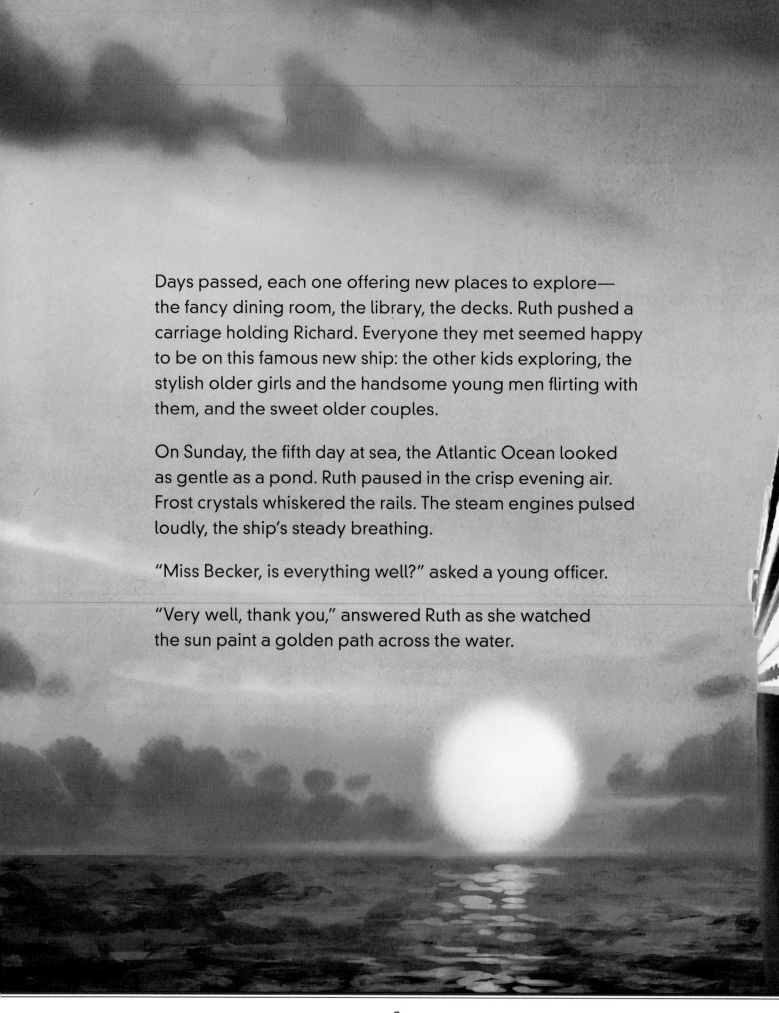

Days passed, each one offering new places to explore—
the fancy dining room, the library, the decks. Ruth pushed a
carriage holding Richard. Everyone they met seemed happy
to be on this famous new ship: the other kids exploring, the
stylish older girls and the handsome young men flirting with
them, and the sweet older couples.

On Sunday, the fifth day at sea, the Atlantic Ocean looked
as gentle as a pond. Ruth paused in the crisp evening air.
Frost crystals whiskered the rails. The steam engines pulsed
loudly, the ship's steady breathing.

"Miss Becker, is everything well?" asked a young officer.

"Very well, thank you," answered Ruth as she watched
the sun paint a golden path across the water.

Just after midnight on Monday, Ruth and Mother woke to silence. The humming engines had stopped. Yelling and footsteps soon echoed in the hallway.

Ruth's mother jumped up and flung open the door. A cabin steward calmed her. "There's just been a little accident and they're going to fix it. We'll be going on in a few minutes."

Ruth lay down, but the engines did not start up again. The ruckus outside their door only grew louder. Hissing steam howled like a siren. What was going on?

About 20 minutes later, another steward appeared at their door.

Ruth rushed to help dress Marion and Richard. Then she draped her coat over her nightdress and stepped into her shoes. In such an excited rush, she forgot her lifebelt.

Ruth and her family trailed the steward up many flights to a deckside room. Other women and children waited there. Some were crying.

WE'VE HIT AN ICEBERG! Ruth heard one woman say.

Some passengers claimed it wasn't safe to board the lifeboats. They could see another ship on the horizon and would wait for it to rescue them. After all, the *Titanic* couldn't sink!

But Mother was adamant. "I want to get off of this ship!" she said.

While officers helped the first-class women and children into the boats, Mother worried about the cold, and she thought there was time. "Ruth, would you run back to our room and get three blankets?" she asked.

Ruth edged against the crowds down five flights to their cabin. Then she made her way back to the deck.

A band was now playing lively music while flares were fireworking in the sky. People pushed, hollered, and searched for family and friends—and news. Who could tell them what was really going on?

Near one lifeboat, Ruth saw officers holding back the men—
even boys about her age. Mothers tried pulling in their sons
and husbands. The men, though, were saying, "Don't worry.
We'll meet you when we're saved by another ship."

Ruth was now glad her father wasn't on the *Titanic*.

Breathless, Ruth reached her mother just as officers were passing Richard and Marion into Lifeboat 11, which was already being lowered down.

"That's all for this boat!" the steward yelled.

PLEASE LET ME IN!
Ruth's mother pleaded loudly.

THOSE ARE MY CHILDREN!

The steward picked her up and dropped her in. As Mother looked up, she saw Ruth still standing on the deck. She shrieked in terror.

Ruth was now alone on the *Titanic*.

From the darkness below, Mother's scream pierced the air,

RUTH, GET INTO ANOTHER BOAT!

Ruth spotted lifeboat 13 being roped down. She zigzagged to a kind-looking young steward. "May I please get in this one?"

"Sure," he said. She was the last person allowed on.

When lifeboat 13 hit the water, it was swept under another boat being lowered.

Two seamen shouted,

ONE! TWO!

They slashed 13's end ropes, and the boat shot free.

On the ship, the band now played slow, prayerful songs. All the lifeboats gone, people lined the *Titanic*'s tilted decks calling for help. Many leaped off, aiming for the fleeing lifeboats. Ruth feared their lifeboat would be swamped.

Some boiler men grasped the lifeboat's oars. They rowed as fast as they could toward safety.

Ruth looked back. The *Titanic*'s port windows slipped slowly underwater, one by one. The ship's lights blazed in the moonless black, the calm sea reflecting them like stars. How strange, thought Ruth, that the ship could look so beautiful, and yet so terrible.

2:20 AM

Then something exploded, a blast rocking the night.

Ruth watched in horror. The front smokestack crashed down, and the *Titanic*'s nose plunged into the sea. A wrenching of metal and wood sliced the ship in half.

Out went the lights.

The rear of the ship rose skyward. Ruth could hear dishes and glasses smashing, furniture crashing, people screeching for help.

The lights flashed on again. The stern stayed up for a minute or so, standing on its ripped end, people falling into the black water.

Then darkness folded them all in, and the ship dropped into the deep.

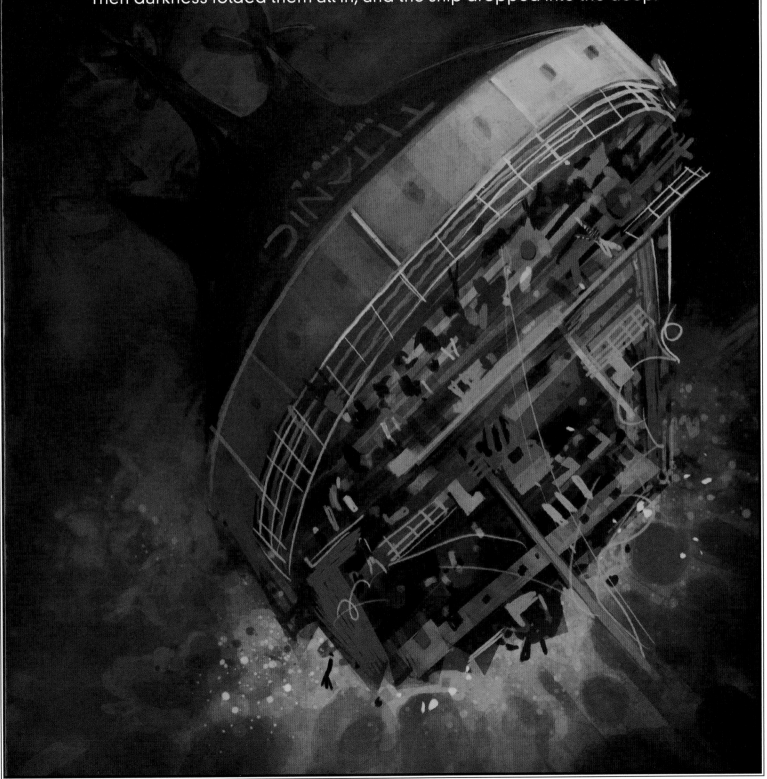

Now Ruth heard the most horrible noise she could imagine—hundreds of people struggling and freezing in the icy water, gasping and wailing for help with curses and prayers.

Ruth could do nothing.

Then, slowly, a deathly quiet blanketed the water. Ruth couldn't turn her mind away from the enormous flock of floating bodies.

Even as the night chill knifed at her own hands and feet, Ruth tore apart her blankets to warm the rowers. When an oarsman cut his finger, Ruth quickly wrapped it with her father's handkerchief.

Gradually the lights of the ship they were rowing toward dimmed ... then vanished.

Ruth closed her eyes and prayed for some sign of hope.

There was nothing but darkness.

The long hopeless hours went on and on the same, cold and cold and cold. Ruth tried to comfort a woman weeping at her side.

Finally, far out in the dark, she spotted a dot of light that grew brighter and larger. Ruth and her boat mates waved and screamed and waved some more. It was a ship! As the dawn glimmered, the men rowed with new energy. Ruth finally felt her hopes rising.

When they reached the *Carpathia*'s side, the others wanted Ruth to board first. Her hands and feet were too numb to climb, so she was lifted in a rope swing. On deck, a crewman embraced her in a blanket.

For nearly four hours, Ruth wandered the ship, searching for her family. Lifeboats straggled in, but not number 11.

At mid-morning, a woman asked, "Are you Ruth Becker?"

"Yes," she answered. Was her family gone?

The woman touched her arm. "Your mother's been looking everywhere for you!"

Mother swooped up Ruth into her arms. Ruth and her family were safe!

But so many were not. Women and children watched for husbands, fathers, sweethearts, children, friends, staff. More than 1,500 people were still missing. The *Carpathia* picked up only 705 survivors.

When the *Carpathia* docked in New York, thousands leaned
toward the survivors with questions, wondering furiously
who had lived, who had died, what had happened.

Everyone wanted Ruth to talk ... but she kept quiet.
It was the heart-numbing quiet of so many lost
in the cold, dark deep.

APRIL 10, 1912	Ruth and her family board the RMS *Titanic* at Southampton, England.
APRIL 14, 11:40 PM	*Titanic* hits an iceberg on the starboard (right) side.
APRIL 15, 12:05 AM	Captain gives orders to get all women and children passengers into lifeboats. Men would follow.
APRIL 15, 1:25 AM	Lifeboat 11, Ruth's family's boat, is launched.
APRIL 15, 1:30 AM	Lifeboat 13, Ruth's boat, is launched.
APRIL 15, 2:20 AM	*Titanic* sinks into the icy sea forever.
APRIL 15, 4:30 AM	Lifeboat 13 reaches the *Carpathia*.
APRIL 18, 9:00 PM	*Carpathia* reaches New York City.

INTERNET SITES

FactHound offers a safe, fun way to find Internet sites related to this book. All of the sites on FactHound have been researched by our staff.

Here's all you do:

Visit *www.facthound.com*

Type in this code: 9781404871434

Check out projects, games and lots more at
www.capstonekids.com

Afterword

As an adult, Ruth Becker taught high school in Kansas and then Michigan. The *Titanic*, though, was not part of her history lessons. No one knew she'd been on it—not even her three children.

In 1982, people started seriously searching for the sunken *Titanic*. New tools could help people explore the sea's bottom.

The deadly quiet in Ruth's head began to be filled with faces and voices, the sounds of people drowning, freezing. She remembered the young men and the fathers, the families from the lower decks, the couples who wouldn't leave each other, the crewmen and workers down below, the kind James Moody who put her on the lifeboat … Perhaps it was time to tell *their* story.

In 1982, Ruth joined other survivors at the Titanic Historical Society's convention to honor the 70th anniversary of the sinking. She let herself remember and tell what had happened on the *Titanic*.

Three years later, the sunken *Titanic* was discovered. Ruth and other survivors begged the world to honor the dead and not take things away from the site. She did not want their grave disturbed.

At the age of 90, Ruth boarded the first ship she'd been on since 1912. Later that year, on July 9, 1990, Ruth passed away. She had asked to have her ashes scattered over the sea, right over the sunken *Titanic*. She wanted to join the others.

On April 16, 1994, she did.